The Pen In Us All

The Pen In Us All

A collection of thoughts
that turned to words
and made their way to paper

FELIX OF MANHATTEN

© Felix of Manhatten, 2015

Published by David Mitchell

Second Edition

 Felixof Manhatten

A CIP catalogue record for this book is available from the British Library.

ISBN 978-0-9932321-0-7

Book layout and cover design by Clare Brayshaw

Prepared and printed by:

York Publishing Services Ltd
64 Hallfield Road
Layerthorpe
York
YO31 7ZQ

Tel: 01904 431213

Website: www.yps-publishing.co.uk

Acknowledgements

Thank you to all those people, friends and family that have, do and will cross my path.

Thank you to all those I have connected with in the past, present and future – we are all on our own journeys.

Thank you all

I would also like to mention the Peninsula hotel in Hong Kong for providing the stage where this particular scene of my life started and where I realised that the "Pen in Us All." is actually an anagram of the Peninsula Hotel (the full stop is the letter "o").

The Virgin Lounge at Heathrow and flight V200 where the notes were written and re-written and a French restaurant called Felix in Manhattan, New York which I have never visited but found when I researched the name Felix of Manhatten.

And lastly a little dog that walked me down a hillside in Hong Kong to find the number 34 bus

To all that read this – "It's your life be Happy"

To write is to love
To love is to share
For you I write and share these precious words
Of feelings and emotions
With meanings to be cherished
For you I write with love

I listen in an instant and hear the ocean calling
As though calling to be together
I listen and can hear the beat of your tender heart
In rhythm, like music with soul

For you, I feel you are my ocean
And can close my eyes and feel your loving soul
A feeling newly discovered
A feeling of joy, that I know will remain

My Ocean, you are so very truly special
Special in so many wonderful ways
With feelings no other can explain
My Ocean, be true and always remember to be you

To write is to love, to love is to share
I will always be there

1

IF

If I had one breath left in my lungs,

If it was the last breath I would breathe

Then I would share it in a kiss with you

If I were to sense an aroma one last time

Then it would be your natural perfume

If I were to see beauty one last time

Then it would be an image of us entwined

If I were to hear angels one last time

Then it would be the sound of your voice in my ear

If I was to sense touch one last time

Then it would be your heartbeat against mine

If I had one breath left in my lungs,

If it was the last breath I would breathe

Then I would share it in a kiss with you

Precious

Precious is time
Time we spend with those we love
Who we care for and who care for us
Time is precious when we are with them or apart
Time is often wasted by not appreciating the moment
We cannot make time
But we can make time for each other
Time doesn't cost anything
But we can spend it too easily
Once spent, it is in the past
We cannot save time for the future
Hold the thoughts time brings
Carry no regrets
Cherish every memory
Live every second
Follow ambition
Recognise opportunity
Build on your hope and dreams
For they are the foundations of your future

To listen is to speak
To write is to read
To be heard is a gift
To write is to express

To speak is to be heard
To read what is written is thoughtful

To reply is to be understood
To do all of these is to be the friend you are

You, me, the universe connected in a perfectly happy happiness

If each grain of sand on earth and each star in the sky were a heartbeat spent with you, a second of time to see your smile

Then the universe is too small for me.

It is expanding and growing to make more stars, planets that have beaches.
It grows to feed my hunger for more time with you.

A second without you is too long; a lifetime with you is too short.

My happiness is all the time between that first second and forever.
We have connected through universal space

The universe of happiness exists because of us,

It is ours to live in and you will never be lost, as I have found you.
You will never be on your own and never be apart, for we have connected.
We are entwined by spirit and soul.
We are together as one wherever our bodies are.
Relax as we know our minds will find each other, pull us together and when they are silent it is because all is at peace, all is tranquil and our separate heartbeats are in harmony for we have found our Happy Place.

You are to me

The feel of your skin,

The touch of your hand,

The beat of your heart,

The breath of your soul.

You inspire me,

You intoxicate me,

The taste of your lips,

Stroking your hair,

The look in your eyes.

Your natural perfumed smell.

Your strength

Your resolve

Your energy

Your youthfulness

With you I have sunshine without you I have rain

Like the ocean without waves

a desert without sand

a forest without trees

a clock without hands

The dawn without the Sun

The night without the Moon

With you

I am a fire with a flame

a mustard field of yellow

a singing bird in a tree

a glass full of wine

You are Me

You mean so much to me

You mean so much to me
You are where I want to be

You are the stars at night
You are the sun so bright

You mean so much to me
You are who I want to see

You make a room go quiet
You turn black to white

You mean so much to me
You are so lovely

You turn dark to light
You make wrong right

You mean so much to me
You are my destiny

You are such a beautiful sight
You are worth every fight

You mean so much to me
You are where I want to be

8

Watching you sleep

I lean across you

Feel your breath against my hand

Caress your cheek

Stroke your hair back across your face

I have found my heavenly place

Watching you dream

Knowing I'm in every scene

Will hold you through the night

Wake up with you in the morning light

And when you're away from me

Can't think of anywhere I'd rather be than kissing you

Where I belong

It's with you I belong
And with you I can't be wrong
I can't answer why, only breathe and sigh
With you I want to stay until I die

We float upon the wings of the butterfly
Into the endless blue open sky
Over the mustard fields' early morning dew
As butterflies we once flew

This is what it's like to love
Open our wings and float above,
The bright yellow mustard field
The start of a new beginning
A future life to build

I write these words for a butterfly
Feel emotion, want to cry

Spring moves to Summer: on the seasons roll
Caterpillar, cocoon, butterfly: around the cycles go

When we are both gone
Those butterflies of you and me
Will be there for eternity

Across the field the first rays of sun come into view
The birds come to life and sing to you
They chirp, whistle and crow
Their love for you continues to grow

Il Mio Solstice Sorriso

We meet but once a year
But your warmth is felt every day

You are the bringer of hope
You rise from the night
You are the giver of life
You are a vision of light

To the darkness of the stars
You are the day's reply

As you rise your finger rays reach down
Lift the dew without a sound
And clear the mist
With your silent kiss

As morning becomes the afternoon
And you are chased by the moon,
I will follow you

Your smiling face
I embrace
Until tomorrow

Be present in the moment

I would trade every memory of happiness,

every minute of hope in an unfulfilled

future just for one moment of the

present looking into your eyes.

Sadhanaspirit

You are a full energetic soul, you exude a free spirit that
enwraps all that is around you.

Your voice caresses the air from your mouth to my ears, it
breathes ideas, images, visions in a silent mantra that grows and
inspires, twines to my thoughts and makes them one with ours.

You are a mirror to me, a reflection of all that I have been all that
I can be all that I will be. You are a silent smile that glows,
a harmony of love that you share with those you touch.

Be strong and true to that reflection as when in doubt you look
into the mirror it will be me who is smiling back.

Rejoice in the time we have been given
and be present in the moment.

Time

Where are we? To whom do we belong?

We are not owned, for we are shared.

We are everywhere, we are everything, we are the someone.
The no one, the everyone.

We feel all that is touched, hear all that echoes, breathe all that is
scented.

See all that there is to see and dream with imagination all we are
blind to see

We are everywhere and we are everything because we are part of
each other, parted in the past, joined in the now and living for the
moment.

Embrace our spirit in support of each other wherever and
whenever it may roam. For you and I are our universe

 Ideas

And when your mind embraces its ideas and dreams and translates them into action, have faith in the fate they will lead you to.

Through the tears that may fall on your path and the smiling sunshine that your presence brings, you will not walk the journey on your own.

Wonder not what waits over the horizon, for you may never get to the horizon. You will always see challenges and opportunities ahead but don't be afraid to stop and look around . Look at where you are, where you have been, for without knowledge of where you have been you have no bearings from which to move forwards.

At times your inner strength will doubt itself but like a flickering candle you will continue to burn, bringing light to those around you and when you need to pass the flame on I will be there to support you, to dispel that doubt, until refreshed you rise to carry the flame yourself. My spirit will be your fuel to go on.

For our flame will not go out. It will not be extinguished, for our minds will continue to burn as a wick, our spirit the energy of the heat and like a Phoenix the ashes will be re-kindled into new life.

So open your heart and soul, let the spirit move you forward, for tomorrow will always be there.

Whenever doubts or pain are in your life, I will always be the medicine that you can take for comfort.

I'm in your mind because you put me there - it is a warm and comforting place and will always be somewhere special.

It has no door, so you never need to knock. It has no windows as you see clarity when you are there.

Your somewhere special has a mirror place in my mind where you comfort me.

In a life where I'm penniless, I will always be thankful for the guidance you give me, which has more value than any coin.

Your friendship is the universal currency of compassion and as such is the richest of all monies. Let us spend what we share as time together and be as one spirit.

Our souls being connected is truly the best bank account there is and one where we will never be overdrawn.

You make me cry smiles of happiness.

39 words to describe you

Awareness, compassionate, emotional, passionate, caring, strength, calmness, motherly, naturist

Persona, natural, Gaia, connecting, loving

Presence, joy, destiny, honesty, truth, empathy, surprise, anticipation,

Charisma, patient, allure, sophistication, flexibility, pure, knowledgeable, vibrant, creative, adaptable

Integrity, engaging, spiritual, healing, wisdom, friendly, awareness, openness, listening

"A thought is a creation in our mind,
we learn to develop happiness"

EE

The leaf of Life

You are the leaf of life,
Often anchored to your tree
At times cast onto the pond of chaos
That maelstrom of change we do not control

You float on
Driven by the change of winds
That dictate your path
You have no shelter from their force,

Your once mill-pond still environment of calmness is replaced by
rippled waves,
You are pushed and shoved, you move from peak to trough.
You rise and fall, occasionally you dip below the surface,
Gasping air in to once again reach upward into the ether

But you cannot drown, for I will not let go of you,
We will swim together against the tide.
We will find eddies to rest in, leeward shelters of sanctuary
And then with strength continue our journey together

Remember you are not alone.

You are never cast away or abandoned

As there is more than one leaf on the tree

And when I see you fall to the pond I will be the first to jump in after you,

I will endeavour to get to the water before you

And cushion the impact

But failing that I will be the breeze that lifts you up

Carries you above the turbulent seas

The one that sets you down in silence,

The one that kisses you on your brow as a sign of security,

The soother to the chaos,

The one that sails you through the tempest of life,

I am the calm at the middle of the storm,

The eye at its centre that will guide you back to the branches of your tree.

TV and Sweets

Nan sat me on my magic carpet, my own island.

Remote in hand, I sat in front of my cinema and controlled the world

Sweets in a bowl, I was self-sufficient in my bubble of fun, excited I flicked through the choices on the TV just as I flicked through the variety of confectionery in my lap.

I was content. I was happy I was in my world. I had anticipation, funny faces and comfort I could laugh and be content in my bubble.

Lighthouse

She stepped in from the darkness and entered her new life She had started her walk at dusk and now in complete darkness she opened the door into her new day. Her inner light shone into the room and she could see - oh how much she could see, a spectrum of opportunity rainbows of hope for tomorrow, paths both challenging and unknown. Her self-belief was her new signpost, her confidence a compass to rely on...

No doubt this story will develop but you will have to write the next chapters. I can only offer you the pencil and paper; it is up to you to write your own future now

Your Future

Create in your mind

Carry in your spirit

Deliver it in your soul

Live it with your heart

10 Ingredients

My ten words for the cake of life

Openness
      Integrity
         Honesty
            Sharing
               Knowledge
                    Questioning
                        Listening
                    Understanding
              Conversations
        Expressing
   Coffee
Loving

To Break Free

We are where we are. We can choose to live as we live, haunted by the fear of change the doubt and insecurity, of what lies ahead.

Listening to the echoing silence of voices from our past, looking for reflections in the shadows they cast.

Each day those shadows get longer until the darkness of the night claims even the shadows. This is the time to rest for tomorrow the newness of new dawn will cast out its golden rays with warmth, energy and hope. Let them embrace you, invigorate you, for today is your future.

Now break free and become your destiny, ride the wave of emotional spirit to carry you over your ocean of anxiety

That Somewhere Place

When I see you, you take me to that somewhere beautiful
That place where there is only you and me

I close my eyes and you walk through my mind
You step through memories; you are the dream to be dreamt

You are endless like a cloudless sky you are that somewhere
beautiful
The tranquillity that exists when silence is all that can be heard,

When smiles cascade from the tree of imagination
When free thought leads you along its branches to our destiny

Our somewhere beautiful is full of fragrances
A perfumed essence of happy joy,

Silhouettes of creativity, painting murals of love across our hearts.
And to lie with you is to be in that somewhere place I now call
beautiful

For it is there that I rejoice in happiness, holding you to my side.
And when I am not with you I can close my eyes and find that
somewhere place

For that place is a place where our souls find the spirit of life

Friend

A friend
Does not judge you on your decisions
or criticise you on you past
they are part of the present
and are there to share the future with you

They are your companions, and are there
at whatever time they need to be

They are never inhibited to give you a truthful reply
or ask any question,
State their own opinion when not asked
and share their true emotions

You know you have a friend when you reflect on their advice,
dislike what they say but accept it

You find time for time together for no reason other than
that you can make that time to be together for each other

You are that friend

You are freedom

You are the smoke that rises from a fire that moves freely skyward

You are the wind that blows the leaves, that bends the trees, the wind that blows the smoke

You are the current that moves the oceans, that breaks the waves that drifts through time

You are not a kite that flies in the sky for a kite is held by a string
You are un-tethered, free to roam, a wheel that endlessly turns no start no end, a constant energy of freedom.

You break no bonds for you have no bonds to break;
Your spirit is free for your soul recognizes no boundaries in which to be held.
You learn through love with a freedom that loves to learn,
Your freedom has no age, only youth,
It is contagious, enriching and overflows your physical entity to become a presence,
A cloak, an aurora of freedom that surrounds you and touches those that share your life.

Your freedom is yours to do with as you choose

Also, know that your freedom brings fulfilment of life to me in the expression of opportunity it opens my mind to.

Be free to be you, for you will meet Jonathan Livingston Seagull on your journey through our Universe to our somewhere place.

Some look inside themselves for freedom. You look outside your soul for life

You fly with the wind not against, it you glide, soar and hover. The breeze flows through your hair like the wisps of air through a bird's feathers.

You take a magic carpet ride over life. You can imagine and pool what you see into a vision you call the reality in which we live and share.

Your brightness burns away all the shadows; all the doubts of darkness evaporate when you speak.

Vocally you bring calmness and serenity to my mind; you bring sense to chaos, hope to challenge, answers to self-questioning.

*"Reflect not on the distance travelled
but on the joy yet to be discovered"*

Artist –
If I was to Paint your Picture

If I was to paint your picture
You would be both subject and canvas

You would always be Work in progress

My emotions would paint you from a
palette of passion,
a rainbow of colours

You would be a constantly evolving
piece of art, a 3-D image of changing
sculptures

You have a presence that resonates, a
sketch, a drawing, you have texture

You are unique to the point that you cannot be painted or copied
but more than that each intimate stroke I made from brush to
paper would be a caress of your skin, my painting would become
you.

I would not be able to distinguish between reality and the picture,
for you are living art, permanently on display in my mind, etched
on the back of my eyes whilst dreaming.

Received post today

Messages in vibes cascaded through my door.
Arms open, hugs of love arrived,
Vibrant, smothered, colourful joy.

A letter of letters combined in an orderly manner that spelt out positive thoughts, reading the words they lodged in my mind.

There they ferment and grow, some will hibernate until liberated by a fresh catalyst, which you no doubt will ignite in my imagination.

The words when read form shapes, smell, textures, a vision from your spirit that joins with mine and dances hand in hand through the fields, towards a future horizon.

A honey filled calmness then takes us on a journey to our next heaven. We just need to agree when?

The message read "thinking of you when you connect to me" which was signature enough to know it was from you.

My first Yoga lesson

And all this from a breath of you.

I breathe an image of you into my lungs lifting me heavenly past whispering clouds of love to join your soul

I continue to ascend passing angels dancing in time to my beating heart, quickening, as I get closer to you.

You reach out your hand to connect our spirits like a raindrop caressing the petals of a flower, refreshing, powerful and bringing fresh life, you guide me into your mind.

We visualize our thoughts into a shared reality which we call our universe. Joyful pictures framed by a destiny we create.

A field with no boundaries, but full of ingredients to sow and grow, trees of imagination, plants of colour, a future of anything we can dream.

It is ours for us and for us it is ours.

And all this from a breath of you.

Dream with me

Go to sleep with positive thoughts and meet me on your journey,
Share a bench, conversations, carrot cake and reality will be our
prize.

Let us swim in a pleasure of mutual ideas that wrap our minds
together, enhance our spirits to a joined destiny.

We will never awake from this state for we will carry the
connection together forever.

Our dreams will become our lives and if you can dream positive
thoughts then our lives will become positive and take us to our
Happy Place.

So sweet dreams and sleep until we meet and let us dream
together until the end of time in our Happy Place.

I Believe In You

I believe in you and the things that you do

I believe in you and who you are
I believe in you and what you want to be
I believe in you. Do you?
Close your eyes to see what lies within
And open your mind to what you can begin

See your future and what lies ahead
Live the moment with no regret
Be strong, be free
Understand what you mean to me

I believe in you and all that you do
And whatever you decide to do
I will stand by you
I believe in you

I am you

Our Journey

We travel the same road
Both on a journey
Sometimes in the same direction
Sometimes not
We leave and arrive at different places at the same time
Sometimes not
But we share our travels.
We remain connected
As distance does not play a part
Our paths are in perfect unison
Aligned by fate and directed to each other
We are a mirror to each other
My right is your left
Your up is my down
But always on our journey
We can hold each other and admire the view
For it is a reflection of our souls spiritually entwined on our
Journey

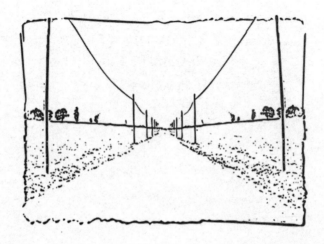

"A bee chooses many blooms, visits
many flowers, tasting all nectars
in order to make it's honey"

The Flower of Manjushri

You are a flower in bloom

And tomorrow you will be a new seed that grows with the new moon

Like a child's soap bubble you will drift in the wind to Manjushri

Where you will settle and be nurtured, thrive and develop.

You will gain strength from all that is around you

The people, the setting, the freshness of the air.

You will reflect on your happiness,

Absorb the energy and nutrition given to you,

The experience, the companionship and love.

Take all that is offered as a flower takes a raindrop to drink

Like a flower opens its petals to hug the sun's rays.
Its roots feel the soil to get food

And you will extend your mind to find spiritual nectar to feed
your soul.

As the flowers colours attract the butterfly, you will become your
own rainbow of joy

Confident, beautiful and passionate to take all your learnings
And paint a new picture for your future, take your canvas of life
and move to your destiny

You are a flower on a journey

Now go and blossom

You are fun

You	are	passionate
You	have	energy
You	have	life
You	give	happiness
You	give	love
You	are	beautiful
You	are	joy
You	care	
You	teach	
You	learn	
You	smile	
You	are	master
You	are	pupil
You	giggle	
You	cry	
You	are	emotional
You	are	special
You	have	freedom
You	have	wisdom
You	are	earth
You	are	wind
You	are	water
You	are	fire
You	are	everything
You	are	wonderful
You	are	all of these to me
And	so	much more

"Take our connected time and treasure what it has brought you as nourishment for the future."

Where you may find me, where you can see me

The flame in your fire
The passion in your desire
The moon in your sky
The tears when you cry
The clouds that hold the rain
The nerves that feel your pain
The hand that wears your glove
The kindness with which you love
The pillow that rests your head
The mattress that makes your bed
The bed on which you sleep
The tissue to hold when you weep

The answers after "why?"
The breath with which you sigh
The ground on which you walk
The words with which you talk
The space in which you live
The joy with which you give
The glass from which you drink
The mind in which you think
The eyes that show the way
The ears that hear the day

The mouth that forms the words
That are cherished when heard
The fingers running through your hair
The nostrils breathing in the air
The blood that flows through your heart
The Karma that we share when apart
The wings on which you fly
The freedom of your sky
Now take these words and what they mean
Dream away and set yourself free

Death

What is death, but a word given when the spirit of one life moves on to embrace another, the transit from one of the universe's rooms to another?

The movement of the soul and mind from the physical entity we call a body?

A body that is nothing more than a skin our soul wears on its journey.

A fashion statement to allow it to experience what some call reality, the real world, but what we know simply as "being."

Death is the start of life, the end of the loop that is the start of a circle,

A passing from here to there, from in to out, from day to night it is the joy of discovery, the acceptance of memories, the knowledge from questions, the learning from teachings.

It is always time to move and I have chosen to journey with you as my companion on our path.

TIME

The hands move across the face

Seconds become minutes

Minutes become hours

Hours become days

Days become weeks

Weeks become months

Months become years

Years become a lifetime

But if I could hold you for just one moment then time would stop

For those sixty seconds would be an eternal moment of happiness.

A moment of purity on our endless journey to bliss.

Share the love of that moment with me as it will give the universe positive energy forever

You are to me

You are the light that lights up my life
You are the food that feeds my love
You are the answer when I am lost
You are the comfort when I need to be held
You are the reason I exist
You are the spirit that guides my mind
You are my reflection in my mirror
You are the colours that make my rainbows
You are the water that fills my ocean
You are the clouds that make my sky
You are the stars that brighten my night
You are the hope that brings my tomorrow
You are the joy that beats in my heart
You are the happiness in my smile
You are the mortar that binds my bricks
You are the flesh that covers my bones
You are the ink that fills my pen
You are the words I write in my book
You are the rain that makes my tears
You are the garden in which I grow

"Tears are the emotional release when we replace ignorance with wisdom"

Your

Look with your eyes
Find with your mind
Kiss with your lips
Make love with your soul
Hear with your ears
Listen with your heart
Talk with your mouth
Speak with your voice
Live with your spirit
Freestyle your life

One person's sunset is another person's sunrise

We create within from without

EE

One mind, two hearts
One soul, two beats
One spirit, two lives
One eternal journey to shared happiness

You can spend a lifetime searching,
just live the moment you are in,
surf the ride that is now,
for that is where true freedom will be found

You are the body
I am the board
Together the shared spirit and soul that is the wave
Freestyle life to the full

Be Your Own Light

Speak of your own experiences,

for they are the things that make us all individuals

Be the joy of our own happiness, for they are the things that make us all smile

Be compassionate with our knowledge, for that is wisdom

Release harmful desires from our minds and replace them with generosity.

Dispel ignorance with wisdom,

Each moment has the potential for enlightenment.

Live in that moment, not the past

Do not place hope in the future, or rely on past memories

Be your own light.

Strolling to discover

She strolls along the beach

She is free

Free as the bird that flies alongside her

Free as the wind that tugs at her hair not covered by her woollen cap

Moisture in her eyes from the cold air

Moisture in her eyes from both the happiness and sadness that her life brings.

Carefree she strolls, her mind both empty and full of thought at the same time.

She turns to look back to the sand to watch the tide cover the prints of her past

And then looks to the future, the beach ahead, virgin to footsteps, a new canvas on which to paint her own future.

To her right up on the shoreline is the debris from last night's storm, the broken, the unwanted abandonment of chaos left and forgotten,

To her left the calm flat waters, framed by a blue cloudless ceiling, on the horizon rises the warmth of the orange sun. The promise of the new dawn.

She strolls along the beach walking the line between the two.

Each grain of sand that takes her step is a crystal of energy from which she gains strength to move forward.

The gull glides effortlessly in unison with her stride as if spurring her on, weaving across her path but guiding her to her own destiny.

Trust your faith, find your truth and be one with yourself

"We all go different ways along the same path but it is who we share the journey with and what we discover that is important"

If you were the sun, the clouds and sky

then I would be the water, ocean and waves,

the land would be where our souls meet,

mirrored in time

We met like strangers do

We met like strangers do,

But are strangers no more
You echo around my mind
Like the wind blowing through the trees.

Images floating, cascading thoughts into view like a
waterfall of energy,
Electric bubbles of smiles pass through the sharp rocks
before plunging into my soul,
Only bursting when they have found that point that will
release their content in a splash of encouragement.

You are the stranger no more.
You have shared your life and dreams,
You are inside me today, forever watching, provoking
thoughts. You are part of my journey, you are part of my
fate.
You are one of the cards that life has shuffled and dealt me,
the hand with which to play my life
You are a catalyst of pure thought, direct and descriptive,
creative and expressive

But most of all I am thankful you are you.

Musical scripts

You glide through the musical script of life
A musician playing each heartbeat as a fresh note that
resonates with passion
Emotions scan as quavers,
Crotchets rising and falling serenading each experience you
encounter
Harmonized friendships compose the reality in which
you waltz
A symphony of compassionate tunes written with pure
thought
A vision of sound vibrates across the page as you write the
next verse of your journey.
Black on white characters stimulate the senses
Sharps become majors as flats become minors
Scores become musical ballets,
A storm of melodies with which you dance through life
Travel to your own beat,
Soul meets spirit as your tempo reveals the true inner you

What if?

The sun had no shine

The clouds held no rain

Caterpillars stopped becoming butterflies

Oceans had no waves

The sky had no stars

Your face had no smile

The birds did not sing

Flowers had no fragrances

Trees had no leaves

What if your heart stopped beating today?

What if we had not met?

Don't live a life of "what if?"

Live a life of DO!

"*A second without you is too long:*

a lifetime with you is too short."

Every day is a solstice of opportunity
A solstice of love
A solstice of freedom
A solstice of choice

That feeling

That feeling
The heartbeat
That tingle
The butterflies
The perfume
That emotion
That ripple of excitement
The anticipation
The stability from chaos your presence brings
All these feelings arise when I see you
All these things arise when I hear you
All these things when I think of you
All these feelings when I am with you
All these things when I touch you
Your comforting voice
Your gentle hand
Your soft breath
Your comforting hand, your soft skin
The freshness and kindness
I wish I could live forever in that feeling

For what will happen?

If tomorrow is the end of the world then spiritually there is no place I would rather be than to be with you, no mind I would rather share, no soul I would want to end this world with but yours.

For all that would happen is we would leave our current forms, our current flesh and blood, that which we call our bodies, and we would drift together eternally in our Universe to find that which we have called our somewhere place.

And I would be happy if the world were to end tomorrow and we drifted together bounded by the strength of the connection we have in this life.

And if we happen to leave this world just one second apart then I would wait on the other side, and yours would be the face and spirit I would look for amongst all those that may pass, and I would wait forever, connected by the memories we have shared.

May your spirit be freed tomorrow whatever happens.

"Life is a tapestry of single threads:
it is how we choose to weave them
together that makes our happiness"

"The greatest obstacle to a Mind is its own ignorance"

The day you met my dad

I'd lost him for many years
But never let him go
You helped me find him on our second trip to say hello

You left us alone and I talked to him
I said "hi," he said "hello". We talked some more
I said "goodbye."
I cried

You held me and told him what a great son he had
I cried
He knew that, but now years later
through your help I knew it as well

You found him a daffodil, knelt down and
planted it next to his rose
With divine flow I released him.
I cried

You then told him we would be back to see
him in flower
We held each other
I cried

I came away and wrote this and cried again, with tears of
happiness not of sadness, tears of thanks to you for bringing us
together.

It was a wonderful day

The day my dad met you

The Ageing Horologist Hands

Hands of mottled skin
Blue veined and paper-thin
Calluses toughened the battles fought
Tradition replaced by digital quartz

Time's hands turn to the future,
my hands adjourn to the past
Springs spring forward, my time has passed
Winter beckons with arthritic pain
Thumbs are numb, phalanges strain
My fingers slowed by my ageing eyes
I have become clock-wise

Hands rigid, my future gone
Time to pass my knowledge on
I need an apprentice to pass on my trade
Second hands to be my aide

Old digits cracked open by the cold
Struggle to grab and keep a hold
Of the coils and gears that move the hands
That tell the time like grains of sand
Falling through the hourglass
Once in the future, now in the past

Surgeon's once operational palms
replaced by limbs no longer calm
Dysfunctional ulna, frictional bones
Metacarpals, radius causing untimely moans
Gnarled ligaments that twist the fingers
No sentiment on which to linger
Cod liver pills to grease the joints
Elderly digits that cease to point

Clockwork, the hands journey on
Second by second a minute's gone
Minutes to hours, hours to days
Round and round in a constant phase
Lubricating oils move the cogs
Sliding mechanisms that tick and tock

And now the death bell finally chimes
The pendulum has swung one last time
Faded time lines that tell a tale
Movements stopped, organs fail
My springs have sprung, my heart just broke
I've been struck by time's last stroke

The Storm

The breeze freshens, leaves depart their host scurrying for cover, skipping over each other in the haste to find refuge, a race of shelf preservation, settling fleetingly before the wind again picks them up and fills them like sails moving them on with another 'you cannot stay here' gust.

The blue sky is highlighted on its edge by a linear swathe of grey, darkening in intensity to the distant horizon. The cold front approaches

Birds stop, devoid of chatter. They move with the leaves to find their haven.
The breeze subsides, a cooler peace now awaits the arrival of the storm, with a quietness that you can hear.

Blue becomes light grey, and then a darker shade paints the sky and moves through into tinges of green and purple, a bruise developing.
The first flash and rumble.
The wound is developing its pain

Large single drops fall, drops that you can avoid. Two drops become three then four. The pavement slabs change from dry, to Dalmatian dots, to a static watery skin that gains energy and flows to the hungry culvert

The waterfall begins, the slabs now replaced by a mirage of upward moving, gravity defying, bouncing drops.
The stream becomes a torrent and flows down the street; the drain issues an 'I'm full' statement and lifts its cover in defiance of the engineer's calculations.

Calm

The colours of freshness appear as a rainbow, blackbirds sing, treading the lawn for worms summoned to the surface by the dropping rain knocking on their roof.

The earthly smell of electrified air flows through your nostrils, stimulates and awakens you.

The bruise's angry rumble moves into the distance.

Then it's gone,

Nature's show moves on, worms be warned.

Oh sweet Celtic voice

Oh sweet Celtic voice
You leave me no choice
I want to hear you again

To see the lips
That sent the words
That made my heart skip,
With what my ears heard

"I'd like to hear you again"

You have a smile that is full and kind
A smile that is as bright as your mind
You have an energy and poise
That brings with it happiness and joy

As your accent deepens and your passion increases you
Start to speak with your eyes
You vocalise with your hands and speak with your Emotionally
driven heart.

And yes, "I'd like to see you again"
Just to hear your sweet Celtic voice

The Girl with the Giggly Spliff

I know a girl with a giggly spliff
Wanders and wonders about all life's ifs
We go for a walk in open park
Step over puddles and talk 'til it's dark
I know a girl who giggles and jokes
Inhales life with a kiss and a smoke
Steps through doors that lie on the grass
Hopes for the future, rolling her hash
She smiles and comments, then giggles again
Dry and warmed with laughter, despite the rain.
She beams and giggles full of joy
Re-lived youth for teenager girl and boy.
Be young be free go with the flow, open your heart and let
your love grow.
They get back to the house where the carrot cake waits
Eat from the box as there's no clean plates.
They have contemplated, chatted and pondered on "being"
And what is reality but all that we are seeing.

In pursuit of happiness

(a photographers view)

Alone she works on "her" shore
Shawl-covered head, she wiles away her loneliness in solitude
Searching her mind to look for an answer
To her emptiness with fortitude

She dreams about whom she will meet
Her cockleshell eyes blindly seeing what she cannot know,
Her thoughts of freedom ebb and flow,
Like the waters below
Her whelk-like feet limpet to the lime green,
Slime green covered rocks
Along the shores of Seaweed Loch

She decants the liquid and pours away her life,
Drifting through the depths of her mind, not a word spoken
Wishing her routine could just be broken
Praying to the moon driven tides to make her a wife
To take her away from the mundane stage
That ties her to this shoreline cage

The bitter salt on the sweet wind blows into her stare
A Gaelic breath that sours the air
She works alone dawn 'til dusk and then retires to bed
Asleep, the ocean returns to leave a fresh green carpet of bread

Like the sea, she will return tomorrow at dawn
But the photographer will be gone

The Vase

Look
At me
And you will see me

Touch me and you will
Feel me

Look inside me to my base
You will find my smiling face

And a kiss from me,
That will belong with you forever

Universal Picture

You are a constant thought in my head,

a permanent mark on my memory.

You are etched like a painting hanging in a gallery,

a portrait of emotional energy veneered to the canvas of my mind.

You are texture, colour, an expression of love, scented when I breathe in.

Sensual to touch, a perfect body that responds with affection and smiles.

You are a torch to the dark.

And you will remain visible to me wherever you are.

You are art in a universal picture of beauty

Student learnings

We insured the car, we taxed the car, then we drove to the lakes
I followed you. You followed me.
I looked in the mirror and you winked back with your broken
headlights. We stopped for oil, I shivered and I poured it on the
road.
It rained and the cars floated north, we sang, tested each other,
then we stopped for oil we were cold and happy.

We arrived we were cold and happy,

Standing on the beach with the wind in your hair, sun in your
eyes and a smile on your face.
Seagulls, happiness, conversation and then I fell over and made
you laugh.
We walked through the woods, talked through the trees, then we
looked for the trunk with a face.

We lost my gloves but found so much more.

You fell asleep, I woke you up. A gentle tap would work better
next time.
We found my standing stones when we were looking for your
stone circles
You wore bags on your feet, I spun the wheels on the car.

We were happy, we were cold.

We shared my first meditation, I cried.
We met others and ate chili lime chocolate mousse at the Charity meal.
I stayed in the wrong room with an empty sleeping bag that wasn't mine. With the window and curtains left open,

I was cold but happy with the warmness you had given me.

We hugged the trees, watched squirrels running. We soaked up the sun and found a Ferrero Rocher tree.
We did world prayer together and sat in the sun. We talked, we connected, we shared. We were happy
We counted 19 steps on the stairs and found the centres at Lima and Mexico, you gave me your book and I was touched.
We are still and always will be happy when we think about those days

We were happy being us

Skywalk with me to our stars

Journeys travelled both near and far
Sail the constellations of love
To the rainbow of planets all above

Paint pictures within your dreams
Of moons and asteroids and what they mean
Take a deep breath and break free
Live your life in what you see

Discover answers with your questioning soul
Gain knowledge and strength from what you behold
Future destiny for us to find
Expand our Universe, expand our mind

Bring openness to an endless sky
Make oneness together and wonder why
Our tranquil place we share together
Where time is meaningless and lasts forever
Timeless are the waves that break upon the shore, an endless
show of planetary force.
Clouds hide where the Angels play, carrying tears upon their
wings, a sadness that they cry as rain to flow back to the sea to
break upon the shore once more
To turn cliff to rock, rock to pebbles and pebbles to sand, grain by
grain to be washed by timeless waves.
And so we have earth, wind and water. All that is missing is the
fire and that is you, for you are the flame that burns in my mind
when I think of you.

Know only what you know

Know only what you teach yourself

Experience and learn from all that you see, feel, smell touch and hear.

Take from others their sentiments but not their judgement. Be true to your spirit.

Doubt others but do not doubt yourself, speak to yourself and listen to your question, for in the question you will find your path.

Take in all around you but only take to heart what truly inspires you, for this is what makes you You.

Cast nothing aside from your mind, just park it for reference later. You are all that you absorb both in your consciousness and your sub consciousness. Learn to soak up the life around you like a sponge and squeeze excess emotions from your body as you cleanse yourself. Exfoliate negatives scrub them away from your body but retain that memory for this will lead you away from darkness and towards the purity of enrichment. Let that process add more to your experience of contentment.

Grow your confidence by being you.

"It is sometimes best to appreciate

the moment we live in and what is

around us than look to a future on an

horizon that we may never get to"

Gaia's Kiss

In anticipation I await

The moisture gathers around me in clouds of expectation.

In excitement I await

The mist envelopes me in purity

Taking my breath away, the gasp of joy as the cleansing starts.

Rivulets fall down my face, accelerating as they descend
Electrifying pulses of life invigorating and massaging their energy
into me

Sensually refreshing, tingling drops of pleasure that caress
warmth in an intense but smoothing massage

An orchestra of harmonies as the cascading waters sing
rhythmically through me, inducing a fragrance of relaxing tones
to my tranquillity.

This is an erotic bliss of joy, to be touched by nature.

Too soon the cloud is emptied and I must turn to the clearing
sky and, naked let the warming sun evaporate the last drops of
moisture from me taking with them the impurity from my soul.

Relaxed the tree lives on.

Oh, the freedom of a kiss from Gaia.

"To contemplate silence is to breathe purity"

Shake off your chains. Break free to roam

Travel your path, the journey is your home
Find all that you can imagine
Dream all that you want to know
Taste all that you want to see
Hear all that can be felt
Smell all that time allows
Exercise your mind
Relax your soul
Stretch your spirits
Enrich your karma
Fulfil your ambition
Discover your destiny
Become your journey
Become yourself
Become
Find your journey
Find yourself
Find
Be your journey
Be yourself
Be
Love your journey
Love yourself
Love
Be love, find love, become love

Hear the silence deafening in your ears

The peace of a heartbeat in unison with life.

An emptiness of peace that spiritually overflows.

To contemplate silence is to breathe purity,

Feel the growing space that your mind moves into,

Filling the voids that were always there,
but which your chaotic life keeps hidden from you

There are no boundaries to this silence,
for this is your own silence - a silence that is within you.

Listen to your mind, listen to your body,
and hear its soul answer with questions.

Your silence needs you to hear your questions, but no reply is
asked for, only the request to contemplate and hear the silence.

Let the silence echo,

let it develop

let it be you

and become at one with it.

"Become the person you are and not the person you think others want you to be"

Positive negative – which are you today?

Positive or negative

Anode or Cathode

Plus or minus

Which are you today?

Which will you be tomorrow?

We measure one to the other

Our highs to our lows

Our trough to our peaks

A start or an end

A challenge or an opportunity

Which will it be today?

Which will it be tomorrow?

Sadness or happiness

A smile or a tear?

They are all choices of our own making,

It is how we choose to react,

Interact or respond that makes us feel positive or negative,

So take a moment and make the choice that makes you feel good.

Positive Mental Attitude

Tuesday morning smile

I open the door

It's Tuesday and I walk into your morning

As the door swings open

You turn your head

Knowing it's me

You raise your eyes from the screen

And smile a 'good morning'

I go to my meeting

'See you next week'

I open the door and leave

'Goodbye 'til next week my Tuesday morning smile'

Reality shifts

We are not in these physical bodies very long and what we do here impacts our continuous life stream. We are great creative beings and if we flow with the spirit within we will create a magnificent world

"the planet at this time is going through huge shifts"

The world exists on many levels and will continue to exist, however the planet at this time is going through huge shifts. This is reflective within our lives.

Be prepared for the structure of reality and how you perceive your world to change. This is the coming of a new age, when one chapter closes so another begins and all that are ready will move into a higher awareness as the illusion falls away we see the light within us.

"this is the coming of a new age"

The galactic community will show themselves and bring an opening in our consciousness.

This has been a long journey and many have fallen but the time is now to see the truth.

Be still within, allow a clear mind and let love flood your hearts for this is truly a wonderful time to be upon this planet, and once the dust has settled the beauty will be nothing like you could ever imagine.

Be free, let go and allow the winds to slowly and gracefully bring you back into alignment with who you really are. Because you are all gods walking the path towards unity.

"you are all gods walking the path towards unity"

Imagine the world within your hearts, fill it with love and place a rainbow around it. Hold this vision with peace and know that whatever happens, release fear and BE LOVE.

There are great times ahead!

Be the wisdom and the knowledge that you seek and all that cross your path will be touched by the presence you hold, and healing will spread far.

It's a time of upliftment, joy and sharing. Let your past go and live in the present, for it is only in your total awareness that you really live at all.

The TRUTH will set you free!

EE

Take the memories that make

the whole complete.

Take the compassion you have and scatter

it as you walk your future path.

May that compassion grow to flourish

in a garden of happiness and love

with each footprint you make.

Let a line of blooming colourful flowers

show where you have walked.

And all that see the path will say.

"That is your path."

If the mind hasn't the capacity to understand then the words stay on the page

EE

Being Grateful

Being grateful is to appreciate what we have,
It's the clothes we wear, not the ones in the wardrobe
It's the food in our stomach, not the food in the fridge.
It's the wine in our glass, not the bottle in the cellar,
It's the smile of our children, not a film on TV,
It's the hug of a loved one, not the argument over nothing,
It's the moment we live in, not a hope for the future,
It's being able to say "I did" not the regret of "did not"
It's the warmth of the Sun, and the crispness of frost,
It's the rain that gives life to the puddles we splash
It's the colours of a rainbow with its promised pot of gold,
It's the imagination to dream that's as endless as time,
It's the sharing and giving, not the taking and wanting.

Being grateful is just "being" happy